Meditations on the ...

AT THE FOOT OF THE CROSS

by J. Lee Magness

STANDARD PUBLISHING

Cincinnati, Ohio

Cover design by SchultzWard

Library of Congress Cataloging-in-Publication Data

Magness, J. Lee.
    At the foot of the Cross : meditations on the Meal
of Remembrance / by J. Lee Magness.
        p.   cm.
    Includes bibliographical references and indexes.
    ISBN 0-7847-0463-5
    1. Lord's Supper—Meditations.   I. Title.
BV826.5.M34   1996
232.96—dc20   96-7301
                                                      CIP

The Standard Publishing Company
A division of Standex International Corporation
© 1996 by The Standard Publishing Company
All rights reserved
Printed in the United States of America
03 02 01 00 99 98 97 96   5 4 3 2 1

Foreword

Where do these meditations come from? They are the result of years of listening and looking while gathered at the Lord's table. They are the result of years of searching the Scriptures, especially in the light of the cross and the meal where we remember it. And they are the result of my own life's experiences and reading about the experience of others, especially those times when I or they have touched the core of faith we find in the cross.

Who are these meditations for? They are for those of you who are called on to instruct the people of God at the table of the Lord. You may want to read them to your congregation just as I have written them. You may want to modify them in small or large ways to fit your circumstances. Or you may want to use them as a springboard to your own reflections. In other words, feel free to make these thoughts and words your own.

But I also hope these meditations will be used by a broader audience. Anyone who wishes to reflect on the cross and ponder the meaning it has for our relationships, our worship, our whole lives may find these beneficial. If you have come upon these meditations because you are responsible for "giving Communion meditations," feel free to find ways of making them available to other members of your congregation. Use these meditations to enrich their understanding and experience of the Lord's Supper, the Lord's death, and the Lord's resurrection.

What are these meditations meant to be? My goal has been a balanced blend of personal experience, depth of scriptural insight, and beautiful language.

Why personal experience? The Lord's Supper is the high point of Christian worship, and Christian worship is the high point of the Christian life. But our actual experience of the meaning of the cross within the life of a worshiping congregation should always be the context of our reflections on it.

Why depth of scriptural insight? If the death and resurrection of our Lord is the highest goal of our reflection, then our reflection should be the most meaningful we can muster. Communion is no time for obscurity, but it is the time for us to be our most thoughtful.

Why beautiful language? If this context—the remembrance of the saving death of our Lord—is the pinnacle of the Christian experience, and this content—the thoughts we think around this table—aims at deep insight, then the words and actions by which we express those thoughts must be our most noble. The language we use at the table must assume the dignity and depth of the occasion. So my words in these meditations are always pushing towards the poetic, not just to be literary, but to convey these concepts in a vehicle worthy of the cargo.

My prayer is that God will indeed enable us to assemble "at the foot of the cross" while we meet around the table of remembrance.

Amelia Earhart Luggage

"When you come together, it is not the Lord's Supper you eat"   (1 Corinthians 11:20).

What would your reaction be if you opened one of the flood of catalogues that inundates your mailbox and, as you thumbed through it, you happened upon a page offering Amelia Earhart Luggage for sale? Or what if you saw it in one of those glossy magazines that are more advertisement than information, or during one of those more-commercial-than-content television programs?

Imagine the possibilities for advertising slogans. "Buy Amelia Earhart Luggage. The luggage that will never wear out even if you're never found!" "Buy Amelia Earhart Luggage. Looks good in the air and under the water!" "Buy Amelia Earhart Luggage. Won't sink even if you do!"

Somehow I think it just wouldn't sell. It wouldn't sell because there is something inconsistent, something contradictory between the name and the product. It would be like offering a line of O.J. Simpson Designer Gloves, or trying to market Richard Nixon Tape Recorders. The name is inconsistent with the product.

We have that same problem ourselves sometimes. We call ourselves Christians and our churches Christian, but sometimes the product is inconsistent with the name.

What about here at this table? This is the Lord's Supper. He inaugurated it, infused it with meaning, instructed us in its use, and commanded its practice. Now he hosts the gatherings around it, and he qualifies the participants.

Its name is "the Lord's Supper." It is "the Lord's Supper." Let us be certain as we gather and as we partake that the product is consistent with the name. Let it be said of us, "When you meet together, it is the Lord's Supper that you eat."

God, help us to remember that this is your table not ours, that we come at your invitation not each other's, and that there is nothing inconsistent about sinners like us being gathered around such a merciful meal.

Seeing Is Remembering

"No one has ever seen God, but God the One and Only, who is at the Father's side, has made him known"
(John 1:18).
"Anyone who has seen me has seen the Father"
(John 14:9).

Has it ever happened to you? Someone asks, "Do you remember so-and-so?" You say, "I remember the name, but I can't remember the individual." They remind you of something the person did. You respond, "I remember when that happened, but I just can't remember the person." Then you run into that individual at the reunion and suddenly, "Sure, I remember you." Seeing is remembering.

Has it ever happened to you? You borrow a book. The description on the jacket sounds interesting. But it is not until you get home and start reading it that you realize, "Heh, I've read this before." Seeing is remembering.

Has it ever happened to you? There is this movie that you know you have seen, but you can't remember a thing about it, not the actors, the characters, the plot, anything. Then, as you watch it again, it all springs back to mind—the characters, the scenes, maybe even the ending. It's like seeing something for the first time and remembering the last time you saw it, all at the same time. Seeing is remembering.

Has it happened to you? You know you have visited that site or that city, but you forget what it looked like. You forget, that is, until you return, and suddenly everything seems familiar: the cottages, the lake, the shops. Seeing is remembering.

It happened to the whole human race when Jesus came among us. We had forgotten the God who had created us and cared for us. But then Jesus came, and when we saw him, we knew God again. Seeing was remembering.

In fact it happens to us every Sunday, when we see that fragment of bread, and the fruit of the vine. It happens to us every Sunday, because as important as the words are—"This is my body; this cup is the new covenant in my blood"—reciting is not always remembering. Seeing is remembering.

God, help us to remember Jesus Christ. Help us to do this in remembrance of him.

Speak for Yourself

"And when he had given thanks, he broke it and said, 'This is my body, which is for you; do this in remembrance of me.' In the same way, after supper he took the cup, saying, 'This cup is the new covenant in my blood; do this, whenever you drink it, in remembrance of me'" (1 Corinthians 11:24, 25).

Speak for yourself! We usually say those words when we disagree with someone. When we want to disassociate ourselves from what he or she has said, we say, "Speak for yourself!"

But there are other forms of disassociation besides disagreement. Explaining something, interpreting it, can also be a form of disassociation. It puts us at a distance, one step further removed, from the idea itself. It may be a helpful distance, giving us another, if not a better perspective. It may be a beneficial step backward or forward, to see the background in context or to notice a minute, but all-important detail.

But however helpful interpretation may be, however opposite explanation may be from disagreement, it still has the effect of distancing us from reality. Sometimes we just need to let the reality, especially the realities of our faith, speak for themselves. And if we do, when we do, we may find ourselves listening to what something really means, rather than listening to ourselves talk about what it means.

Today let's just say to the Lord's Supper, "Speak for yourself." Let's let the emblems speak for themselves—bread and fruit of the vine, grain and grape, cracked and crushed, emblems of life, of life in death. And let's let the actions of the meal speak for themselves—taking and thanking, blessing and breaking, pouring out and sharing among, waiting, recognizing, remembering. And let's let the words speak for themselves—"This is my body broken for you," "This is my blood of the new covenant poured out for many for the forgiveness of sins," "Do this in remembrance of me."

God, help us to let this meal speak for itself in our lives, and to let this meal speak to others through our lives.

This Meal, Every Meal

"Taking the five loaves and the two fish and looking up to heaven, he gave thanks and broke the loaves. Then he gave them to his disciples to set before the people. He also divided the two fish among them all. They all ate and were satisfied, and the disciples picked up twelve basketfuls of broken pieces of bread and fish. The number of the men who had eaten was five thousand"

(Mark 6:41-44).

"When he had taken the seven loaves and given thanks, he broke them and gave them to his disciples to set before the people, and they did so. They had a few small fish as well; he gave thanks for them also and told the disciples to distribute them. The people ate and were satisfied. Afterward the disciples picked up seven basketfuls of broken pieces that were left over. About four thousand men were present"

(Mark 8:6-9).

"While they were eating, Jesus took bread, gave thanks, and broke it, and gave it to his disciples, saying, 'Take it; this is my body.' Then he took the cup, gave thanks and offered it to them, and they all drank from it. 'This is my blood of the covenant, which is poured out for many,' he said to them"

(Mark 14:22-24).

———————

There is a sense in which every meal, mundane or miraculous, has been a foreshadowing of this meal, memorializing the gift of life in his death. The recognition of the gift of God's grace in this meal reminds us that in every meal we must recognize the gracious gifts of God.

And there is a sense in which this meal, this lordly Supper, both mundane and miraculous, sanctifies every meal, making each one a celebration of life through this death. The regular recognition of God's gifts for which we express thanks each time we eat reminds us of the inexpressible gift we recognize around this table.

God, there is no question that we will take and break, eat and drink; now we ask that you help us to remember Jesus whenever we do.

The Foot of the Cross

"You see, at just the right time, when we were still powerless, Christ died for the ungodly. Very rarely will anyone die for a righteous man, though for a good man someone might possibly dare to die. But God demonstrates his own love for us in this: While we were still sinners, Christ died for us" (Romans 5:6-8).

They stood at the foot of the cross. They stood but did not kneel. Their eyes were squinting to slits in the noonday sun, squinting like the sightless pretending to see. These men were blinded by years of looking through glasses tinted with law and tainted by sin. They were blinded by years of looking for the wrong Messiah for the wrong reasons. With their eyes so set on a sovereign to save them from their servitude, they could not see the Sovereign in the Servant.

They stood at the foot of the cross. They stood but did not kneel. How ironic were their words! They named the criminal, "the King of the Jews," accurate in spite of their spite, inaccurate in the light of his heaven-and-earth authority. They threw his words back at his mute mouth, "Aha, the one who would destroy the temple and rebuild it in three days," and the feat they thought impossible was happening right before their eyes. They called his bluff, saying, "He saved others, let him save himself," not realizing that to really accomplish the one, he could not do the other. Then they said, "Let him come down from the cross, so that we might believe." This was the final irony, since we believe precisely because he did not come down from the cross.

Here we are gathered, around this table, as close to the foot of the cross as we dare to get, care to get, need to get. And we wag our heads in wonder, not that he died, but that he died for such as them, and for such as us, standing at the foot of the cross.

God, help us to look at the cross with while-we-were-yet-sinners eyes.

The First Meal
on the Moon

"And he took bread, gave thanks and broke it, and gave
it to them, saying, 'This is my body given for you; do
this in remembrance of me.' In the same way, after the
supper he took the cup, saying, 'This cup is the new
covenant in my blood, which is poured out for you'"

(Luke 22:19, 20).

Over twenty-five years ago Neil Armstrong
hop-stepped from a metal ladder to the dusty-
gray surface of the moon and said, "One small
step for man, one giant leap for mankind." The
first man on the moon! How wonderful, that in
the midst of all those wonders of technology—
booster rockets and guidance systems and
lunar landing modules—it all came down to
one human step.

Many of us remember the first man on the
moon, but do we remember the second man on
the moon? We are aware of that first step on
the moon, but what about the first meal on the
moon? That second man was Buzz Aldrin, and
that first meal was the Lord's Supper.

Buzz Aldrin had taken bread and wine, still
common in spite of their consecration, from
earth to ether, in little NASA plastic contain-
ers. Here's what he said later about it: "In the

one-sixth gravity of the moon, the wine curled slowly and gracefully up the side of the cup. It is interesting to think that the first food eaten there were the elements of Holy Communion."

How wonderful, that in the midst of all the wonders of technology—shrink-wrapped, vacuum-packed, barely-recognizable-as-food—it all came down to bread and wine, grace-full wine. How wonderful, that across all the expanses of time and space (and I do mean space)—across two hundred and fifty thousand miles and twenty centuries—the elements remain so simple, so much the same. How wonderful, that it all comes down to one sip, one supper, one bite of bread, for the man on the moon and for us.

God, help us to remember that nothing, least of all time and space, can separate us from your love in Christ Jesus.

Cold Bread
and Warm Wine

"When he was at the table with them, he took bread, gave thanks, broke it and began to give it to them. Then their eyes were opened and they recognized him, and he disappeared from their sight. They asked each other, 'Were not our hearts burning within us while he talked with us on the road and opened the scriptures to us?' They got up and returned at once to Jerusalem"

(Luke 24:30-33).

———————

"They got up and returned at once to Jerusalem." This is just one of the wonderful statements in Luke's account of the appearance of the risen Lord to the two people on the road to Emmaus.

What's wonderful about it is that these two had been worrying all weekend about their Christ-turned-corpse, then wearying their way to their walk's end, seven dreary miles home. Then they barely sat down for a bleary-eyed meal with the Stranger, when he became a soaring sight for their eyes. In an instant he was gone from their sight, and they were hop/skip/jumping their way back to the future.

Why did they decide on a sudden return to Jerusalem? The answer is that the resurrection of Jesus has that kind of impact. It caused them to leave the bread and the wine, to get up and go all the seven miles back. It caused them to forget about the lateness and the darkness as they resumed their traveling. It had that kind of impact.

It is at this table that we recognize Jesus; it is here that we present the reality of the risen Jesus. And that the reality of the resurrection, recognized most clearly here, makes us get up and return at once to whatever city of doom or despair we have dragged ourselves here from, and say, "It is true, the Lord is risen!"

God, thank you for asking us to come and sit at a meal that makes us so able, so eager, to jump up from it with joy. Help us to live in the reality of the resurrection.

In Memory of Him, In Memory of Her

"While he was in Bethany reclining at the table in the home of a man known as Simon the Leper, a woman came with an alabaster jar of very expensive perfume, made of pure nard. She broke the jar and poured the perfume on his head. . . . And they rebuked her harshly. 'Leave her alone,' said Jesus. 'Why are you bothering her? She has done a beautiful thing to me. . . . She did what she could. She poured perfume on my body beforehand to prepare for my burial. I tell you the truth, wherever the gospel is preached throughout the world, what she has done will also be told, in memory of her'" (Mark 14:3-9).

In Jerusalem they gathered for a meal, Jesus and his disciples. Jesus took a loaf and shared it with his guests. Then he took the cup and shared it with his guests. He told them, "Do this in memory of me."

Just a night or two before, in nearby Bethany, a wealthy Pharisee and Jesus and other prominent guests gathered there for a meal. In slipped a woman who poured expensive ointment on Jesus' head. When the disciples protested, Jesus said, "Wherever the gospel is preached, this will be told in memory of her."

What did she do that was so special, that deserves to be remembered? Why should her deed be commended in language similar to that used at the Lord's Supper: in memory of him, in memory of her?

When others were haughty, she was humble. When others spoke their appreciation, she acted it out. When others hid under a sin-thin veneer of respectability, she repented.

But ultimately she deserves to be remembered because she remembered him. She would smile through all her pain if she knew that our remembering her makes us remember him.

Today, as we break this bread and share this cup, let us remember him by remembering her who remembered him.

God, help us live repentantly, in memory of her, and help us live redemptively, in memory of him.

A Crossword Puzzle

"For all have sinned and fall short of the glory of God, and are justified freely by his grace through the redemption that came by Christ Jesus"
(Romans 3:23, 24).

———————

There's a crossword puzzle in the Gospels. That is, there's a puzzle in the words Jesus spoke from the cross.

At the moment of his death he was talking about the life of others: "Father, forgive them, for they know not what they do."

At the moment of his rejection as a supposed rebel he was talking about the repentance of a revolutionary: "Today you will be with me in paradise."

At the moment of the dispensation of the ages he was talking about the disposition of his aging mother: "Dear woman, here is your son." And to John, "Here is your mother."

At the moment of personal defeat he was talking about spiritual triumph: "It is finished."

At the moment of his greatest personal tragedy he was talking about his great personal trust: "Father, into your hands I commit my spirit."

There's a crossword puzzle in the Gospels,

but there's also a crossword puzzle in this meal. That is, there's a puzzle in the words we speak about this memorial of the cross.

We celebrate life in him while we talk about his death: "This is my body broken for you."

We remember and repent of the sin that broke our relationship with God while we talk of its restoration: "This cup is the new covenant in my blood."

It's a crossword puzzle in which every answer is "grace." Since "all have sinned and fall short of the glory of God," they "are justified freely by his grace through the redemption that came by Christ Jesus."

God, we thank you for filling in the blanks of our empty lives, for solving the puzzle of our sin, for saving the puzzled, for turning us towards the cross.

The Last King
of the Hawaiians

"The Word became flesh and made his dwelling among
us"   (John 1:14).
"And they sang a new song: 'You are worthy to take the
scroll and to open its seals, because you were slain, and
with your blood you purchased men for God from every
tribe and language and people and nation'"
                                    (Revelation 5:9).

———————

The depictions of the ancient Hawaiian
kings are all over the island. They had almond-
shaped eyes and skin dark as koa wood and
cheekbones as precipitous as a crater's edge.
And they all wore the royal robe—a cape
woven of tiny red and yellow feathers, plucked
from little tropical birds they would trap and
release.

Anyone who knows what a Hawaiian king
looked like would have recognized the figure in
the stained glass window in the Palapala
Hoomau Congregational Church on east Maui.
He had the eyes, the cheeks, the skin; the long
black hair and the short black beard; and, of
course, the red and yellow cape.

But it was not King Kamehameha—the
First, the Second, the Third, or the Fourth!
It was King Jesus, with his downcast eyes

and his down-reaching hand.

The figure in the window sheds light on the incarnation. It reminds us how the glory of God had been filtered through flesh, how in Christ God became one with us, whether Jews, Hawaiians, Japanese, or Caucasians.

This meal is also a window on the incarnation. In it we celebrate the fact that in Christ God not only came among us but became one with us, in life and in death and in life again.

So when we say, "This is his body broken for you," and "This cup is the new covenant in his blood," we are reminding ourselves that God became like us. He was a flesh-and-blood, infant-adolescent-adult, live-till-he-died human being. And we are reminding ourselves that God came among us, all of us, whoever we are and however different from one another we are. This is his body, broken for all of us. This cup is the new covenant in his blood, reconciling us to God and to one another.

God, we praise you and thank you now for the good news that what you accomplished in Jesus Christ was nothing less than that the Word should become flesh and dwell among us, all of us.

Go and Learn
What This Means

"While Jesus was having dinner at Matthew's house, many tax collectors and 'sinners' came and ate with him and his disciples. When the Pharisees saw this, they asked his disciples, 'Why does your teacher eat with tax collectors and "sinners"?' On hearing this, Jesus said, 'It is not the healthy who need a doctor, but the sick. But go and learn what this means: 'I desire mercy, not sacrifice.' For I have not come to call the righteous, but sinners'" (Matthew 9:10-13).

Suppose the kindergarten teacher admitted only geniuses into his class. Then most of us would never get an education.

Suppose the doctor agreed to see only healthy people in her office. Then most of us would never get well.

Suppose Jesus had come to call only the righteous. Then most of us could never follow him.

Suppose God did require a personal sacrifice from us for salvation. What offering could we make that would ever remove our offense?

But now, think about the Lord's table. Suppose it was only for those who had neither disappointed nor disobeyed nor doubted their Lord. Then most of us—no, all of us—should pass the bread by unbroken, and watch our reflections in the cup pass before us undrunk.

Suppose we refused even to gather at the Lord's table because we judged ourselves guilty. Then we would be truly guilty, not of sin, not of unrighteousness, but of refusing to come, to follow, to eat, as sinners.

Mercy, what presumption! Not only to reject our relationship with God by sinning, but to reject our reconciliation with God by thinking that this meal is not precisely for us who are sinners. Mercy!

Go and learn what this means: "This is my body given for you. This is my blood of the covenant, poured out for many for the forgiveness of sins."

God, give us the wisdom and the humility, to let you doctor us not just because we are sick, but even though we are sick.

And Eat With You

"Here I am! I stand at the door and knock. If anyone hears my voice and opens the door, I will come in and eat with him, and he with me" (Revelation 3:20).

Jesus spoke those words, those red-letter words. He is the "I," standing at the door. As he is standing, he is knocking on the door, and calling through the broad boards of the door. He is the one standing there sad-eyed and thorny-crowned, knocking with raw knuckles cupping a pierced palm. He is calling as if from the broad beams of the cross, except for the fact that he is standing at the door, knocking.

But on whose door does he knock? To whom does he speak? Not to the lost, but to the found. Not to the loyal, but to the lukewarm. He speaks to the Christians of Laodicea, who were well-clothed but naked, eagle-eyed but blind, prosperous but pitiful, and neither hot nor chilly cold. They are Christians, but he must threaten to spit them out of his mouth.

And what does he want with them, the luke-warm-like-us Laodiceans? What does he want with us? Not just to hear, not just to open, not even just to come in and stand there in awk-ward, don't-I-remember-you-from somewhere silence. He comes to eat with us, to eat with us, and us with him.

These words from Revelation are not about conversion, but about Communion. They are not about finding Christ for the first time, but about being found by Christ again and again. They are not so much about salvation, as about supper-time, Lord's-Supper-time.

Listen! He is standing at the door, knocking. If we can hear his voice and tear open the door as we tear that morsel from the loaf, he will come in to us and eat this meal with us, and us with him.

God, help us to make this meal the open door policy of our lives.

An Elegy for Easter

"A week later his disciples were in the house again, and Thomas was with them. Though the doors were locked, Jesus came and stood among them and said, 'Peace be with you.' Then he said to Thomas, 'Put your finger here; see my hands. Reach out your hand and put it into my side. Stop doubting and believe.' Thomas said to him, 'My Lord and my God!'" (John 20:26-28).

————————

Happy Resurrection Day! This is his body broken for you.

Happy Resurrection Day! This is the blood of the covenant poured out for you.

Why do we let the blood-dark memory of his crucifixion intrude on our celebration of the resurrection? Why do we have the Lord's Supper on Easter Sunday? Why have an elegy in the midst of a rebirth-day party?

Because when the risen Lord raised his resurrected hands, the scars of the spikes were still visible. Because when he invited his followers to confirm in their own minds the reality of the resurrection, he did not suggest that they touch his hair, his nose, his fingers, cracked from years of labor as a carpenter, his arms hard as the hardwood he had worked.

He did not point out the familiar marks of

his life, but the cruel, horrible marks of his death.

And so we must allow the blood-dark memory of his crucifixion to intrude on our celebration of the resurrection.

Happy Resurrection Day! This is his body broken for you.

Happy Resurrection Day! This is the blood of the covenant poured out for you.

God, help us to see the light of his resurrection more sharply in the shadow of his death.

Everyone Is Equal

"Jesus said to them, 'The kings of the Gentiles lord it over them; and those who exercise authority over them call themselves Benefactors. But you are not to be like that. Instead, the greatest among you should be like the youngest, and the one who rules like the one who serves. For who is greater, the one who is at the table or the one who serves? Is it not the one who is at the table? But I am among you as one who serves'"

(Luke 22:25-27).

"It is not easy for Christians from the outside world to understand this. But a long while ago, we made a decision to be a holy people, setting ourselves apart for the cause of the gospel. . . . I have been made the Responsible Brother for a period of three years. . . . I pray. . . . I study the scriptures. . . . I examine the faith of the believers. . . . At the service, I cease to be the Responsible Brother. Before the direct presence of God, every one is equal. . . . Every worship is a communion service: Christ speaking to his disciples. That is why we have a twenty-minute period of silence before communion. Any one of us can break bread."*

We have many things to learn from our Chinese brothers and sisters in Christ, not the least of which is their understanding of the Lord's Supper.

They remind us that "every worship service is a Communion service." The Chinese Christians sing hymns of praise to God as we do. They pray and listen to the proclamation of the Bible as we do. But the heart of their service is Communion. And so it should be for us. They also remind us that worship means listening, listening to God. We are good at speaking to God. Our hymns and prayers are meaningful expressions of our praise and petition. And we are very good at speaking about God as we discuss his revelation in the Bible. But Communion is something different, something special. It is "Christ speaking to his disciples." It calls for listening, and listening calls for silence. And so it should be for us. And the Chinese Christians remind us that around this table "everyone is equal," equally famished, equally filled. Even the Responsible Brother sits down to serve and be served. And so it should be for us.

God, as we gather at this table, we empty our eyes of all but the cross. We close our lips and open our ears to your word of grace. We grasp the hands of the brother and sister with whom you have graced us in Jesus.

*from *Households of God in China's Soil*, Raymond Fung, ed.

Food, From First to Last

"When they landed, they saw a fire of burning coals there with fish on it, and some bread. Jesus said to them, 'Bring some of the fish you have just caught.' Simon Peter climbed aboard and dragged the net ashore. It was full of large fish. . . . Jesus said to them, 'Come and have breakfast'" (John 21:9-12).

———————

First thing after he first called them, they ate together, at a water-to-wine wedding feast at Cana. Last thing before he died, they ate together, a body-bread, covenant-cup supper in the upper room.

First thing after he rose, they ate together, Jesus and the two grief-eyed men of Emmaus, a bread-breaking, eye-opening-at-last meal. Last thing before he ascended, they ate together, Jesus and his glory-eyed disciples, Jesus and his you-will-be-my-witnesses, goggle-eyed disciples.

Early in his ministry he ate with the hungry Galileans on the gravelly shore. Later in his ministry he ate again, this time with the hungry Gentiles on the grassy slope.

First thing, last thing, after our resurrection, we eat together, the marriage supper of the Lamb.

From first to last, what we do here today,

breaking this bread and drinking this cup, has been done in one way or another every yesterday and will be done in one way or another every tomorrow. From first to last, the eating we do here today, we will continue to do until today says yes to yesterday, until today has no more tomorrow. From first to last, the eating we do here today, is the pattern of the past and the occupation of eternity. Let's eat!

God, we thank you for these artifacts of antiquity, these emblems of eternity. We ask that they may give us renewed meaning for this moment.

Making Room for Jesus

"Then came the day of Unleavened Bread on which the Passover lamb had to be sacrificed. Jesus sent Peter and John, saying, 'Go and make preparations for us to eat the Passover.' 'Where do you want us to prepare for it?' they asked. He replied, 'As you enter the city, a man carrying a jar of water will meet you. Follow him to the house that he enters, and say to the owner of the house, "The Teacher asks: Where is the guest room, where I may eat the Passover with my disciples?" He will show you a large upper room, all furnished. Make preparations there.' They left and found things just as Jesus had told them. So they prepared the Passover" (Luke 22:7-13).

———————

Who was that man, nameless in the gospel narrative, but willing to share his house? Did he know the Teacher well or at all, or was he only known by Jesus? Was it his servant or his son that the disciples spied, as they scratched their heads, eyeing averted eyes, searching the swollen city for who-knows-whom?

Had Jesus and the owner of the house arranged a signal? A man bearing a water jar would have been an eye-catching figure. It was against all current convention, for usually women were the carriers of water. Was the water for washing feet, poured and pooled in the bowl still by the door, left to lap at the lip of the basin, until the host played household servant?

Why did Jesus speak as though it were his "guest room"? Had he roomed there before, and now made reservations with reservations, leasing it for the least of these his brethren?

And how did it come to be furnished and ready? Did this unnamed owner know, when he folded the towel, and set the low table, and scattered the cushions, who would be using them? Was he even dimly aware of what words of horror and hope would ring round that room, what deeds of service and symbolism would be enacted there?

Do we? Do we know what will come of our actions when we make room for Jesus? We have perhaps come to this table a thousand times. It would be possible for us to make our way through this meal with our eyes closed. But we want to do more than go through the motions, because we know something very wonderful is happening here.

God, we pray that you will help us to make room for Jesus, to make ourselves furnished and ready for this Communion with him.

He Broke It

"For I received from the Lord what I also passed on to you: The Lord Jesus, on the night he was betrayed, took bread, and when he had given thanks, he broke it and said, 'This is my body, which is for you'"

(1 Corinthians 11:23, 24).

He broke it. When we, like Jesus, break the bread, we are participating in an act at once simple and significant. A fellow Christian from Japan writes: "Here is a strong image of the 'broken Christ' in the ancient Christian apostolic tradition. This broken Christ, indeed, confronts us. But he goes further than that. By being broken he indicates to us the new possibility of embracing others. In my judgment here is the great spiritual message of Christianity to humanity. One must be broken in order to embrace others. . . . When the bread is broken, there is created a space between the two pieces of bread. This space is sacred. This Eucharist space is the space in which the divine embracing of sinful humanity takes place."*

We have heard those words many times before—"he broke it." But Kosuke Koyama hears them a little better. He hears them with the ears of a child who experienced the firebombing of Japan. He hears them with the ears of a missionary to the urban poor of Thailand. He sees them with eyes that have beheld the brokenness of human life and how the broken Christ not only heals but embraces this broken world.

When we break bread together today, let us look not only at the speck we eat, the emblem of the body of our broken Lord. Let us also look at the space, the sacred space between one piece and the next. In that space God embraces us and others, all others, in his saving love.

God, we give thanks for your embrace which we remember in the face of the brokenness of Christ. And we ask that you help us to become the kind of people who embrace the brokenness about us.

*from Kosuke Koyama, "The Asian Approach to Christ," Missiology 12:435-447.

Her Own Share

"Jesus called them together and said, 'You know that the rulers of the Gentiles lord it over them, and their high officials exercise authority over them. Not so with you. Instead, whoever wants to become great among you must be your servant, and whoever wants to be first must be your slave—just as the Son of Man did not come to be served, but to serve, and to give his life as a ransom for many'" (Matthew 20:25-28).

―――――――

We ought to remember, more often than we do, those who give of their time and effort to prepare the Lord's table for us every Lord's Day. But one Chinese woman gave of more than her time and effort. Her husband writes:

"We have always had floods. Immediately after the Liberation, three flood control dams were built. . . . But then things turned bad. . . . [I]n 1964, we had two weeks of continuous rain. When the water burst through, it could not be stopped. It wiped out everything in its path. . . .

"Food was scarce. . . . Of course Christians also went about on empty stomachs. . . . In 1966, my wife passed away. She had been eating very little, letting me and the boys eat. . . . She died of starvation. We held a service to remember her. I did not officiate until towards the end when the Lord's table was set. As I reached into the jar for the dry, thin biscuits, I realized there weren't enough to go round. My wife who made these biscuits had always seen to it that there was enough for everyone. . . . I still cannot figure out how she had managed to provide enough biscuits for the Lord's table when food was so scarce—unless she had added her own share."*

The story is a poignant and powerful reminder of the One who not only gave his share, but gave himself. He not only died so that we could eat, but died so that we could live. There is even a sense in which those among us who prepare this bread and cup every Sunday can stand as humble reminders of the One whose body was broken and whose blood was poured out for our sakes.

God, help us to remember, as we gather at this table, that our Savior came not to be served but to serve. Help us to do the same.

---

* from *Households of God in China's Soil*, Raymond Fung, ed.

Mary's Baby, Mary's Body

"And she gave birth to her firstborn, a son. She wrapped him in cloth and placed him in a manger, because there was no room for them in the inn"

(Luke 2:7)

"Near the cross of Jesus stood his mother, his mother's sister, Mary the wife of Clopas, and Mary Magdalene"

(John 19:25).

Frances Frank has written these haunting words about Mary, the mother of Jesus:

Did the woman say,
When she held him for the first time in
   the dark dank of a stable,
After the pain and the bleeding and the
   crying, "This is my body; this is my
   blood"?

Did the woman say,
When she held him for the last time in
   the dark rain on a hilltop,
After the pain and the bleeding and the
   dying, "This is my body; this is my
   blood"?*

I don't know if Mary said those words or not, as the poet suggests, either at Jesus' birth or at his death. But she had every right to do so. She had given him life.

41

We don't have that right, but we do have that privilege. Not because we gave him life, but precisely because he gave us life.

So when we break and share this bread, let us, each one, say, "This is my body"—that is, his body broken for me. And when we pour and share this cup, let us, each one, say, "This is my blood"—that is, his blood poured out for me.

God, help us to consider his body so carefully here today that we become his body more completely here today.

---

*Frances Croake Frank, in *Distorted Images*, ed. Anne Borrowdale

Michelangelo's Masterpiece

"I eagerly expect and hope that I will in no way be ashamed, but will have sufficient courage so that now as always Christ will be exalted in my body, whether by life or by death. For to me, to live is Christ and to die is gain" (Philippians 1:20, 21).

It isn't the ceiling of the Sistine Chapel, but it's a masterpiece. It isn't "The Last Judgment" on the wall at the end of that great hall but it's a masterpiece. It's a simple, little masterpiece by Michelangelo.

It's only a sketch, a pencil sketch, a red-pencil sketch, a double red-pencil sketch. On it one scene, a resurrection, is sketched over another scene, a burial. They were drawn together by the same artist with the same pencil on the same piece of paper. And they must be drawn together: the death-demanded burial, and the red-dawn-drawn resurrection.

But although the burial scene is plainly the burial of Jesus, the resurrection is not his. It is one he performed: the resurrection of Lazarus.

Why did the master piece the death and burial of the one who would rise to eternal life together with the resurrection of one who would rise only to die again? We do not know.

But we do know that the death and burial of Jesus was not just for himself, for the one who died to live. It was for those of us who live in the shadow of the grave, all us "Come-forth!" Lazaruses.

This meal is not only the remembrance of Jesus' death and burial acted out in glib anticipation of the happy ending of his resurrection. It is the remembrance of his death and burial reenacted in the realization that we who have been called into new life in Christ will yet die in Christ. And it reminds us that we who will die in Christ will yet live in him.

It reminds us to join with Paul in saying, "For to me, to live is Christ and to die is gain."

God, we who are about to die salute you, and we who are about to live celebrate you.

Publicans and Sinners

"While Jesus was having dinner at Levi's house, many tax collectors and 'sinners' were eating with him and his disciples, for there were many who followed him. When the teachers of the law who were Pharisees saw him eating with the 'sinners' and tax collectors, they asked his disciples: 'Why does he eat with tax collectors and "sinners"?'" (Mark 2:15, 16).

"He eats with tax collectors and sinners." To the Pharisees it was an accusation. To think, that the one who claimed to be the Holy One of God would eat, would share this sacred moment of human communion, with the unholiest horde of humanity! These were greed-tainted tax collectors, who served the enslaving Gentiles! These were promiscuous prostitutes, the unclean, the people of the earth-under-their-fingernails! It has always been true—He ate with sinners. But it was never truer than at the last supper.

There was Judas, his knuckles white as he clutched his money bag close to his chest. Was it now thirty silver pieces fuller?

There was Peter. He was the one to whom Jesus said, "Get thee behind me" and, "Put your sword away." He was the one who said of Jesus, "I never knew him."

There were James and John, hot-tempered as a summer storm. They were the ones who wanted to call down fire upon an obstinate Samaritan village. The ones who clamored for the best seats at Jesus' side in his kingdom.

There was Matthew, the (dis)honest-to-goodness tax collector.

There was Simon, the militant, the take-matters-into-his-own-bloody-hands revolutionary.

They were all there, all the disciples, sinners if not tax collectors, and he ate with them.

It reminds us that, if we ever come to this table without recognizing that we are sinners, we are making a grave mistake. For "if we claim to be without sin, we deceive ourselves and the truth is not in us" (1 John 1:8). But it also reminds us that, if we ever fail to come to this table because we do recognize ourselves as sinners, we err. For "if anybody does sin, we have one who speaks to the Father, in our defense—Jesus Christ the Righteous One. He is the atoning sacrifice for our sins" (1 John 2:1, 2).

Whenever we eat this bread and drink this cup, we celebrate the fact that he still eats with people like us.

God, help us in this meal to see our sin more clearly, and our salvation more clearly, because we have seen his sacrifice more clearly.

Remembering Blue

"In a little while you will see me no more" (John 16:16).
"Because I live, you also will live"   (John 14:19).

Late one Thursday afternoon the young man phoned his eighty-seven-year-old neighbor, "Blue" Hyder. They talked for a long time. They talked about death and about how Blue's brother had pretty much given up on life. He had quit eating and did not talk much. "He'll die soon," Blue said. But they also talked about life. They discussed the earlier-than-ever daffodils in Blue's yard, and how he'd already cleaned off the tomato cages for spring planting.

The next morning about 8:30 or so, Blue finished his customary breakfast of fried egg and toast, sat down in his easy chair, and died. When the young man talked to Blue's family later that day, he found himself rehearsing that phone call of the previous day, that phone call about death and about life. Somehow those last words became an important contact with Blue's death and celebration of his life.

Late one Thursday evening the disciples talked half the night with Jesus. They talked about death. They conversed about how Jesus wouldn't be eating with them any more and how they wouldn't be seeing him for a while. He would die soon. But they also talked about life, about how he was the life and about how since he lived they would live in him. The next morning he was crucified, and by the afternoon he had died.

After Jesus died, those who knew him, and those who came to know him, told and retold the story of that evening. They rehearsed over and over again that conversation about death and about life. Somehow those last words became their contact with his death and their celebration of his life.

And they still are. When we break this bread and drink this cup, we recall his words, "This is my body." "This is my blood." And in this way we come into contact once again with his death and with his life.

God, we thank you for the way these intimations of life banish the intimidation of death.

Where Would He Sit?

"When he noticed how the guests picked the places of honor at the table, he told them this parable: 'When someone invites you to a wedding feast, do not take the place of honor. . . . For everyone who exalts himself will be humbled, and he who humbles himself will be exalted'" (Luke 14:7, 8, 11).

If Christ came to Communion, where would he sit, and what would he do? Would he first find the front, so that he who was first-born and first fruits would be the first served?

Would he preside, striding to the front uninvited yet unrestrained? Or would he rise only at someone's insistence, to instruct us on the depth of his death, on the mystery of the meal?

Would he instead serve at the table, patiently, purposefully passing the Body of Christ bearing the Body of Christ to the Body of Christ?

Would he have prepared the meal, baked the bread, and poured out the fruit of the vine, filling each cup with care?

Would he clean up, wiping away the leftovers of the merely miraculous meal, rinsing the remnant of wine out of each cup, rubbing off the red crescent sticking to the lip?

Or would he have been the one who had

winnowed the wheat, ground the grain, and gathered the grapes? Would he be the Sower whose plowing and planting and plucking we take so for granted as we dig in?

If Christ came to Communion, what would he be: guest, host, or servant? What would he do—prepare, preside, pass out, or clean up?

I suspect he would at least be what he at last was—the host. Oh, not the host at the head of the table, but the host here on the table—Body broken, Christ crushed.

God, help us to take seriously being served this day, as if by the one who came not to be served. Help us also to take seriously serving every day, as if in the name of the one who came to serve.

A Role for Real

"Therefore, I urge you, brothers, in view of God's mercy, to offer your bodies as living sacrifices, holy and pleasing to God—this is your spiritual act of worship. Do not conform any longer to the pattern of this world, but be transformed by the renewing of your mind. Then you will be able to test and approve what God's will is—his good, pleasing and perfect will"

(Romans 12:1, 2).

The powerful World War I novel, *All Quiet on the Western Front,* became a popular motion picture in 1933. The lead role was won by an up-and-coming actor named Lew Ayres. Many people all over the world have read the novel, many have seen the film, and a few may even remember the promising young actor.

But most people do not know that the experience of acting out the horrors of that war transformed Lew Ayres. He became convinced that he could not with a clear conscience kill another, even in warfare. So when World War II broke out, he filed for and received conscientious objector status and promptly volunteered to serve as a chaplain and medic on the European front. In spite of his sacrificial service, Ayres's decision ruined his movie career. When the war was over, no one would take a risk on this conscientious objector whose role in a movie had become real in his life.

We too have been cast in a drama, a play about a great battle between the forces of sin and death and salvation and life, the reenactment of the death of Jesus. When we break this bread and share this cup, we show forth, we demonstrate, we act out, his death until he comes again.

The question is, will playing this role become real in our lives? Will reenacting his death transform our lives? Will it make us new people with new priorities? Will we find ourselves not only playing our part in the drama of this meal, but living out the life-giving principles of our Lord in the face of the death-dealing principles of our age?

God, we pray that as often as we eat this bread and drink this cup we will reenact his death until he comes again. And when it comes to living your life in our lives, may it be more than play-acting.

The Medicine
of Immortality

"A man ought to examine himself before he eats of the bread and drinks of the cup"   (1 Corinthians 11:28).

Have you ever been sick, so sick you went to the doctor, so sick she gave you one of those knock-it-out-of-you-once-and-for-all shots or some of those knock-you-out pills?

And while you lay there awkwardly on the examining table, did she try to explain to you what the drugs were and how they worked in your body?

Perhaps you lay there thinking that you weren't really in the mood for listening to all this. You may have decided that even if you were you couldn't have conjured up enough high-school biology to understand her explanation. And you probably concluded that whether or not you understood, the medicine would have the same wonderfully healing effects.

Now we come to the Lord's table, which is, according to Paul, a kind of "examining table." We come now to eat the Lord's Supper, which some of the earliest Christians were fond of calling "the medicine of immortality." It's an interesting phrase. It implies an illness and a cure; it implies that the meal can heal.

Ever since those early days Christians have been trying to explain just what this meal is and how it works. And in the midst of our sometimes spiritual sicknesses and fevered states we have tried to listen to their explanations. We have wrestled with terms like "transubstantiation," "consubstantiation," "real presence," "symbolic presence," and "mystical presence."

But I'm not sure that even if we understood this meal better it would "work" any better. Or to put it another way, I am sure that "the medicine of immortality" would still have its same wonderfully healing effects.

We may not understand it completely when we eat this bread and drink this cup, but we are certainly better for having eaten.

God, we thank you for the honest diagnosis of our sin, and for the prescription of salvation though your Son.

Main Course, Leftovers, or Appetizer?

"For whenever you eat this bread and drink this cup, you proclaim the Lord's death until he comes"
(1 Corinthians 11:26).

Just what is it we are eating here, as we gather around this table? Is it breakfast, lunch, or supper? Is it a morning coffee break or an after-Sunday school snack? Hopefully, it is not a bedtime snack. If it truly is "supper," is it the appetizer or the main course or the dessert? Just what is it we are eating here, as we gather around this table?

There is a sense in which the food we are about to eat at this table is the main course, the meat and potatoes of our experience of worship. It is the moment in which, by eating and drinking, we celebrate our salvation.

But there is also a sense in which the food we are about to eat at this table is the leftovers. It is the last course of a long-ago meal, not warmed over but warmed up week after week and tastier than ever. It is the moment in which, by eating and drinking, we reenact the last supper meal that prepared for our salvation.

And there is also a sense in which the food

we are about to eat at this table is only the appetizer, a pretaste, a nibble, a whiff of the aroma of the main course, the marriage supper of the Lamb. It is the moment in which, by eating and drinking, we preenact the meal that consummates our salvation.

God, we pray that this meal, whether appetizer or entree or dessert, will be for us the spiritual nourishment we have gathered to find.

Last Words and the Last Supper

"Father, forgive them, for they do not know what they are doing" (Luke 23:34).

Jesus had come to forgive, and he died forgiving. When we gather at this table, we recognize and accept that we are forgiven, and we recognize and accept that we must be forgivers.

"Today you will be with me in paradise."

Jesus had come to save, and he died saving. When we gather at this table, we recognize and accept the salvation that comes from him. We acknowledge that because He has saved us, we must be with him wherever and whenever. We recognize and accept his call to be sharers of salvation.

"Dear woman, here is your son." "Here is your mother."

Jesus had come to make community, and he died forging a new family. When we gather at this table, we recognize and accept our place in a new network of relationships, a new family of faith and fellowship and service.

"My God, my God, why have you forsaken me?" "I am thirsty."

Jesus had come to teach, and he died teaching, quoting messianic prophecies from

Psalm 22, pointing to the predictions of his death. When we gather at this table, we too teach, showing forth his death until he comes again.

"It is finished."

Jesus had come with a mission, and he died with his mission on his mind. When we gather at this table, we recognize that we are people with a mission, on a mission, with him and with each other.

"Father, into your hands I commit my spirit."

Jesus had come with trust in God, and he died trusting. When we gather at this table, we recognize and accept his death, and death itself, in the light of our trust in the God who gives life.

God, as we gather at this table, help us to forgive the enemy, love the outcast, care for the community, teach the truth, be faithful in ministry, and trust in you.

Scripture quotes are from Luke 23:34; Luke 23:43; John 19:26, 27; Matthew 27:46; John 19:28; John 19:30; Luke 23:46.

Know, Remember, Preach

"For I resolved to know nothing while I was with you except Jesus Christ and him crucified"

(1 Corinthians 2:2).

"Remember Jesus Christ, raised from the dead"

(2 Timothy 2:8).

"But we preach Christ crucified" (1 Corinthians 1:23).

Three scattered Scriptures come together to form a powerful triad in our thinking about the Lord's Supper. First Paul tells us he determined to know Jesus Christ. In the second Paul exhorts his young cohort to remember Jesus Christ. And third, Paul declares his intention to preach Jesus Christ.

There they are: know Jesus Christ, remember Jesus Christ, preach Jesus Christ.

To know Jesus Christ is more than mental assent. It is the experience of a lifetime, his and ours. It is the experience of his life in our lives, and of our lives in his life.

To remember Jesus Christ is more than to know Christ. It demands the regular, ready recollection of the resurrected one in our own daily dying-to-live life. This includes, but is not limited to, this weekly meal.

To preach Jesus Christ is more than to remember Christ. It is the living proclamation of the one who we may reverently say was dead as a doornail. He entered the dominion of death so that we might be transferred out of the kingdom of darkness into his marvelous death-shall-have-no-dominion light.

But one of the most fascinating things about these three commands is that we can carry out all three at once in the eating of this meal.

When we eat, we discern the body of Christ. It is here, around this table, that we know Jesus Christ.

When we eat, we do so in remembrance of him. It is here, around this table, that we remember Jesus Christ.

When we eat, we proclaim the Lord's death until he comes again. It is here, around this table, that we preach Jesus Christ.

So we eat this bread, recognizing his body broken for us. We drink this cup, recognizing the new covenant in his blood. And as we do so, we are knowing, remembering, and preaching Jesus Christ.

God, we pray that you help us do this in remembrance of him, in full knowledge of him, and as proclamation of him.

A Holy Meal,
a Human Meal

"By this time it was late in the day, so his disciples
came to him. 'This is a remote place,' they said, 'and
it's already very late. Send the people away so they can
go to the surrounding countryside and villages and buy
themselves something to eat.' But he answered, 'You
give them something to eat.' . . . Taking the five loaves
and the two fish and looking up to heaven, he gave
thanks and broke the loaves. Then he gave them to his
disciples to set before the people" (Mark 6:35-37, 41).

The words were simple, the actions mundane. He took; he blessed; he broke; he
poured; he spoke; he gave. But on Jesus' lips
the words became profound, and at Jesus' fin-
gertips the actions became sacred, humans
participating in the holy.

The words, no matter how often repeated,
are still simple. The actions, no matter how
often reenacted, are still mundane. We take;
we bless; we break; we pour; we speak; we
give. But spoken in the name of Jesus even our
words become profound, and done in the name
of Jesus even our actions become sacred,
humans participating in the holy.

The words were simple, the actions mundane. He had them sit down on the grass, He

took bread and fish, He gave thanks, and He gave it to the disciples. They in turn gave it to the crowd.

The words are still simple, the actions still mundane. We see the hungry, and we are led to set aside what we possess in abundance. Then we give thanks, divide it, and give it to those who will give it to others who hunger.

And spoken and done in the name of Jesus our words become profound and our actions become sacred, humans participating in the holy.

God, may this meal, this holy meal that you have given us, become our model for feeding others in your holy name.

His Blood Be on Us

"When Pilate saw that he was getting nowhere, but that instead an uproar was starting, he took water and washed his hands in front of the crowd. 'I am innocent of this man's blood,' he said. 'It is your responsibility!' All the people answered, 'Let his blood be on us and on our children!'" (Matthew 27:24, 25).

Pontius Pilate dishonestly declared, "I am innocent of this man's blood. It is your responsibility!" And then he sent Jesus to his death.

The crowds at least answered honestly: "His blood be on us and on our children!" There is a sense in which we can and should say the same words, the words of the crowd, when we gather at this meal to commemorate his death. We say, "His blood be on us," because we have accepted our guilt, and we have felt our shame.

But there is another sense in which we can and should say those same words, but for a completely different reason. We say, "His blood be on us," precisely because his blood has removed our guilt, and we are freed from our shame. So when we are tempted to cringe in horror because our sin caused the shedding of his blood, let us instead cry out with joy because we are washed in the blood of the Lamb.

And so we say, "His blood be on us," as a way of remembering his sacrifice. We say, "His blood be on us," as a way of repenting of our sin. We say, "His blood be on us," as a way of rejoicing in his salvation.

God, may his blood be on us and on our children, not just as a result of our guilt, but in recognition of your saving grace.

Feeding the Corpses

"But because of his great love for us, God, who is rich in mercy, made us alive with Christ even when we were dead in transgressions—it is by grace you have been saved" (Ephesians 2:4, 5).

The brothers fed the stray cat that showed up periodically at the back door. They gave some attention to the cows who happened to live in the field next door. But an ant farm was their first official pet. They tried to follow the supposedly simple instructions as best they could. They assembled the plastic case, poured in the white grains of sand substitute, and gently installed the colony of ants. They fed them the right stuff in the right amounts at the right time.

But one by one the ants died—all of them. The older brother was disappointed by the demise of his first true pets. But the younger brother stared at the sad scene and offered a solution: "Let's just feed them some more and they'll come alive again."

The parents smiled wistfully at the wishful thinking of the youngster. They unceremoniously dumped the contents—white pellets, ant corpses, and all—out in the back yard, and put the empty ant farm on the shelf where you keep things you should throw away but can't.

But isn't that exactly what God did for us? Didn't he "feed the corpses" so that they came back to life? "God . . . made us alive with Christ even when we were dead in transgressions."

And we commemorate that event, the making alive of those who were dead, the "feeding of the corpses," every time we gather at this table. One thoughtful early Christian writer called it the "medicine of immortality." A child might call it "the food you give them so they'll come back to life." We call it "Communion."

What are the simple instructions for this feeding? The first step is to take the bread and give thanks for it and break it and share it and think, This is his body broken for me. The second step is to take the cup and give thanks for it and drink it and share it and think, This cup is the new covenant in his blood.

God, we thank you for your mercy: for wanting us dead or alive, for making us alive even though we were dead.

The Feast of Regeneration

"See! The winter is past; the rains are over and gone. Flowers appear on the earth; the season of singing has come, the cooing of doves is heard in our land. The fig tree forms its early fruit; the blossoming vines spread their fragrance" (Song of Songs 2:11-13).

———————

Over eight hundred years ago, in the middle of the twelfth century, a great Russian preacher, Cyril, Bishop of Turov, preached a beautiful and meaningful sermon on the resurrection.

Spring had finally come to his cold land. But he could not think about spring without thinking of the resurrection. And he could not think about the resurrection without thinking of what he called the "feast of regeneration." Listen to what Cyril wrote:

"Last week there was a change of all things, for the earth was opened up by heaven. . . . Today the heavens have been cleared from the dark clouds that enshrouded them as with a heavy veil, and they proclaim the glory of God with a clear atmosphere. . . . Today the sun rises and beams on high, rejoicing warms the earth, for there has arisen for us from the grave the real sun, Christ, and he saves all who believe on him. . . . Today the winter of sin has stopped in repentance, and the ice of unbelief is melted by wisdom. Today spring appears spruce, and enlivens all earthly existence; the stormy winds blow gently and generate fruits, and the earth, giving nurture to the seed, brings forth the green grass. For spring is the beautiful faith in Christ which, through baptism, produces regeneration. . . . Today there is a feast of regeneration for all the people who are made new by the Resurrection of Christ."

Listen again to Cyril's last statement: "Today there is a feast of regeneration for all the people who are made new by the Resurrection of Christ." "Today"—this every-first-day-of-the-week resurrection day—"there is a feast of regeneration"—this feast, these emblems of death which exude the energy of life—"for all who are made new by the Resurrection of Christ"—all of us people who are risen to walk in newness of life.

Springtime has come! He is risen from the dead! Take and eat!

God, help us see resurrection in every spring, in every Sunday, and especially in this feast of regeneration.

Familiarity Breeds . . .

"When he was at the table with them, he took bread, gave thanks, broke it and began to give it to them. Then their eyes were opened and they recognized him" (Luke 24:30, 31).

———————

Why is it that so often when Jesus appeared to his followers after the resurrection he was eating? It happened in Jerusalem and in Galilee. It also happened in Emmaus. Why was he always eating?

It may be because we see each other, the real each other, best at mealtime, at the point of our common need, in the midst of a common act.

And why is it that Jesus the invited guest suddenly became the host in Emmaus? He had been invited by another man to come into that man's house to eat his food at his table. Why was Jesus acting as the host?

It may be that Jesus had a way of becoming the host even when he was the guest, preferring to serve rather than to be served.

And why was it that they recognized him when they did? He was no longer merely companion or questioner or teacher, but breadbreaker when they realized it was he? Why?

Some think they saw for the first time the

strange scars on his bread-breaking hands. But perhaps they saw something not strange but familiar, the familiar hands going through the familiar motions. Had they seen him break bread for the five thousand, for the four thousand, for the twelve in the upper room?

We've all done this before, this breaking of the bread, this taking of the cup. Every Sunday for every year for who knows how many years, we've done this over and over. Some might say that such familiarity would breed a kind of contempt.

But that does not have to be true in this case. This is a familiar setting, a meal. It calls to mind a familiar role for Jesus, serving. We are about to participate in a familiar act, breaking the bread, drinking the cup. Familiarity breeds . . . recognition. He is known to us in the breaking of the bread.

God, we pray that our holy habit might continue to make this meal more not less. We pray not for repetition but for recognition.

Bringing in the Cross

"But I, when I am lifted up from the earth, will draw
all men to myself"   (John 12:32).
"For whenever you eat this bread and drink this cup,
you proclaim the Lord's death until he comes"
                                (1 Corinthians 11:26).

A Chinese Christian woman gave the following testimony of faith centered in the cross:

"The cross has been the centre of our lives
and of our meetings. This wooden cross,
hand-carved for us by a kind young man, is our
fifth. . . . You see, we always begin our meetings, as in the old days, with the cross coming
into our midst. This way we feel the heavenly
Father is with us.

"Yes, this wooden cross, I think, is our fifth.
The first was silver, my family's cross. It came
in very useful when, towards the end of the
fifties, Pastor Pi lost his church and asked my
husband if he and others could use our home
for prayers. . . . With him the cross was always
the centre. . . . At some time during this period,
the silver cross was stolen. . . . I was able to
locate another cross, an ivory one. . . . We met
around the ivory cross.

"Then the Cultural revolution came upon
us. One day, my neighbour's 14-15 year-old

son . . . came to my door and quietly tipped me off about 'a house confiscation' visit by the Red Guards any time. . . . My husband . . . told me to get rid of the ivory cross. So I hid it in the charcoal pile in the kitchen. Three days later they arrived. . . . They found my ivory cross with ease. The leader took it right in front of me, moved his young head in mock pity, let the cross fall and crushed it with his foot. . . .

"I decided to make a small cross for myself. . . . I carried it all the time in my pocket, touching it and remembering Jesus.

"There are now over forty of us in our Thursday meetings. And we've got a bigger cross, hand-carved by one of our young people. [W]e let him bring in the cross."*

These words from our Chinese sister in Christ remind us that the cross must always be at the center of our lives. She reminds us that, when we break this bread and drink this cup, we "bring in the cross," showing forth his death until he comes again. She reminds us that to touch the cross means to remember Jesus.

God, as we come to this meal, help us to understand our eating and drinking as a way of "bringing in the cross."

---

*from *Households of God in China's Soil*, ed. Raymond Fung

Birth and Death

"For God so loved the world that he gave his one and only Son, that whoever believes in him shall not perish but have eternal life. For God did not send his Son into the world to condemn the world, but to save the world through him" (John 3:16, 17).

Ignatius, a Christian leader from Antioch, wrote these words in about A.D. 110:

"A star shone forth in the heaven above all the stars; and its light was unutterable, and its strangeness caused amazement; and all the rest of the constellations with the sun and moon formed themselves into a chorus about the star; but the star itself far outshone them all; and there was perplexity to know whence came this strange appearance which was so unlike them . . . , when God appeared in the likeness of man unto newness of everlasting life. . . . " (To the Ephesians, 19).

Ignatius wrote these words about a birth, about life, on his way to his death as a martyr in Rome. Ignatius wrote these words about the Bethlehem sky full of stars while he was on his way to a Roman stadium full of beasts. And Ignatius recognized that the star of stars not only signaled incarnation—God appearing in human likeness—it also signaled eternity—

"the newness of everlasting life."

We gather today, commemorating birth and death. We celebrate the coming of the incarnate Christ and the presence of the crucified Christ, all in this one act of worship.

This is his body, once that of a tiny baby, but later broken for us. This is the cup of the covenant in his blood, a covenant that led from Christmas to the crucifixion.

And when we partake, we do so in celebration of his birth, in remembrance of his death, and in anticipation of life, everlasting life.

God, we take these tokens of his death as a token of his birth and, not less, of our own as well.

The Beauty of Golgotha

"Carrying his own cross, he went out to the place of the Skull (which in Aramaic is called Golgotha). Here they crucified him, and with him two others—one on each side and Jesus in the middle" **(John 19:17, 18).**

Have you ever been struck at how many horrible things have happened in such beautiful places?

Think of the mystery and beauty of the Central American rain forest. Here we envision the too-green-to-be-true foliage, flowers blooming like freeze-frame fireworks, and birds pluming in a dash-splash of color. Then watch the fire raid turn that paradise of feather and frond into a bare, brown, bloody graveyard.

Think of buildings white as a cloud in a clear sky, of a pale-as-emerald, clear-as-crystal sea, and of towering green cedars on the towering white mountains of Lebanon. Then watch the mortars crack the mortar and crush the homes, while the sea fumes and foams with smoky-black refuse, and the mountains moan and mourn under the bombs.

Sometimes the most horrible things—like death and destruction—can happen in the most beautiful places.

Golgotha on the other hand may have been a singularly horrible place. It was surely stamped and stippled by the studded sandals of the soldiers, scarred and scored by the countless crosses dragged across it. And it must have been marked by empty poles and holes, like the sockets of a skull. The Place of the Skull would have been a horrible place.

But sometimes the most beautiful things can happen in the most horrible places. May this meal remind us of the beautifully horrible thing that happened in that horribly beautiful place.

God, grace our lives, however horrible our circumstances, with the beauty of your grace.

The Case of
the Missing Meal

There's a mystery in the Gospel of John. It's in chapter thirteen. It's the mystery of the missing meal. Oh, there's a meal going on all right, the same upper-room supper we read about elsewhere, but the meal is missing. There is not one word about the broken bread or the covenant cup, no this-is-my-body, no this-is-my-blood. It's the case of the missing meal.

But there are clues, telltale marks of the meal all around the room. We might say there are footprints and fingerprints and voiceprints that give evidence, incontrovertible evidence, that the Lord's Supper is hidden there somewhere in the last supper.

There is the clue of the footwashing. It featured a basic basin with a towel rubbed, rinsed, and wrung. Then Jesus spoke the words, "If then I have washed your feet, you also ought to wash one another's feet."

Clue number two was Jesus' response to Peter's brash brush-off: "If I don't wash your feet, you have no part in me."

Then there is the third clue, their consternation at "Where I am going you cannot follow now," followed by their relief at "but you shall follow afterward."

And finally, like the echo of a whisper, clue four: "By this shall all people know that you are my disciples, if you have love for one another."

There they are: clue one, sacrificial service; clue two, participation in Christ; clue three, anticipation of future life in his presence; and clue four, shared love and shared life.

It is there after all, there where it apparently is missing, in John 13. The case of the missing meal is solved whenever we gather around this table. It is solved by our own commitment to sacrificial service, by our participation in Christ's death, by our hopeful anticipation of his return, and by our love for one another.

God, help us see the significance of this meal everywhere we look, and help us see your Son every time we meet at this meal.

Communion
and Community

"They devoted themselves to the apostles' teaching
and to the fellowship, to the breaking of bread and to
prayer. . . . Every day they continued to meet together
in the temple courts. They broke bread in their homes
and ate together with glad and sincere hearts"

(Acts 2:42, 46).

They devoted themselves to the breaking of
bread. And day by day they broke bread in
their homes. Unless Luke, the author of the
book of Acts, is being uncharacteristically
redundant, he is reporting on two important
and intertwined activities pursued by the earliest Christians. His first reference seems to be
to what we call Communion, the Lord's Supper.
The second appears to be a reference to community meals. If so, they took both activities
very seriously, Communion and community.

And why not? These two characteristics of
the Christian life cannot exist without the
other. Communion must take place in the community of believers. It was never meant to be a
solitary thing, a kind of microwave meal for
one eaten in isolation from others. And community, Christian community, must always be
centered on Communion. The fellowship of the

saints would not even exist if God in Christ had not transformed us through the very event this meal commemorates.

The earliest Christians took both Communion and community every seriously. And so must we.

We fellowship not only with the Host, the Savior, but also with the other guests, the saved. We celebrate the death of his body on the cross, and we celebrate the life of his body, the church. Whenever we gather, even two or three of us, we gather in his name, knowing that the crucified and risen Lord is in our midst. Whenever we remember his death, we must be conscious that his blood was poured out for the person next to us as surely as for us.

Let us devote ourselves to the breaking of bread. But let us also break bread in our homes, with glad and generous hearts.

God, help us to enrich our Communion by a consciousness of our community. Help us also to enrich our community by our consciousness of Communion.

Here and Now

"But we sailed from Philippi after the Feast of Unleavened Bread, and five days later joined the others at Troas, where we stayed seven days. On the first day of the week we came together to break bread" (Acts 20:6, 7).

You are here at the right place. And you have come now at the right time. There is no one for whom "here" is the right place and for whom "now" is not the right time. This table is the right place for each of us. What we are about to do here now is done at the right time for each of us.

If we lack understanding, this is where we begin to remember. If we lack fellowship, this is where we begin to become one. If we have sin in our lives (and who doesn't?), this is where we meet mercy.

We may have lost our focus, or perhaps we feel we have lost touch, and our lives have become insipid. This is where we begin to see Christ again, touch Christ anew, taste Christ afresh.

You've come to the right place, at the right time. This is where Jesus took bread and gave thanks for it, broke it, and gave it to them, and to us, saying, "This is my body broken for you." This is when Jesus took the cup, gave thanks for it, poured it out, and shared it with them, and with us, saying, "This is the blood of the new covenant, poured out for many."

This is the right place for us, right here. And this is the right time for us, right now. We are here now, right where and when we need it most, and need each other most, and we need him most.

God, we thank you not only that we are here at the right place and at the right time, but also that you are here, in these elements. And we thank you for Jesus in whom you came in the fullness of time.

Priests Before God

"As you come to him, the living Stone—rejected by men but chosen by God and precious to him—you also, like living stones, are being built into a spiritual house to be a holy priesthood, offering spiritual sacrifices acceptable to God through Jesus Christ. . . . But you are a chosen people, a royal priesthood, a holy nation, a people belonging to God, that you may declare the praises of him who called you out of darkness into his wonderful light" (1 Peter 2:4, 5, 9).

———————

You probably think we have gathered on this first day of the week for a worship service. After all, there would be no worship without that first-day-of the-week resurrection. But when the early Christians of Troas gathered on the first day of the week they didn't just gather for a worship service but for a Communion service—to break bread. After all there would be no resurrection without the crucifixion.

But suppose if someone told you that you were gathering here today for an ordination service—your ordination service. Would you think someone had made a mistake?

Every worship service, especially every Communion service, is an ordination service. When we ordain individuals to Christian ministry, we set them apart to a life of teaching, helping others to remember the past, to remember Jesus Christ. We set them apart to a life of preaching, proclaiming Jesus Christ, crucified and risen, present and real in our lives. We set them apart to a life of comforting, pronouncing hope in the face of death, promising life through the one who died.

But each of us has been set apart to ministry, each of us who makes up that royal priesthood. And each time we gather about this table we participate in those very ministries that some are set apart to perform. We teach by remembering Christ, by reenacting his saving story. We preach by proclaiming Christ, by showing forth his saving death. And we comfort by sharing the promise of His coming again.

God, help us partake today not only as penitents, recipients of your grace, but as priests, ministrants of your grace.

Rejoicing or Repenting?

"Is not the cup of thanksgiving for which we give thanks a participation in the blood of Christ? And is not the bread that we break a participation in the body of Christ?" **(1 Corinthians 10:16).**

It is hard to know what best to call it—this meal we gather to share. Is it not Communion? Yes, it is—a participation in the body of Christ our Lord and Communion with the body of Christ, the church. But it is also Eucharist, thanksgiving. Giving thanks at this table is not merely the mindless repetition of the words, "and he gave thanks and broke it." It is the cry of our hearts, echoing Paul's cry: "Thanks be to God for his inexpressible gift!" And this meal is also the Lord's Supper, or more accurately, the lordly supper. It is here, gathered around this table, at the foot of the cross, where we learn best his lordship.

But in a sense the name we call this meal— Communion, Eucharist, Lord's Supper—is secondary to the attitude with which we come to it.

Do we come remembering that we are a part of Christ because he made himself a part of our lives? Are we remembering that we are a part of the body of Christ, the fellowship of the faithful, the society of the saved?

Do we come rejoicing that the one whose life defied death opened the way to life beyond death? Are we rejoicing that we whose lives deserve death have through his death been given life?

Do we come repenting, not only in the light of our weakness but also in the sight of his greatness? Are we repenting by being called up to our knees before our Lord?

Perhaps it wouldn't hurt to call this meal by all its many titles Communion, Lord's Supper, Eucharist—to remind ourselves that we must come to it remembering and repenting and rejoicing.

God, help us to move beyond the mood of the moment; help us to repent and rejoice as we remember.

We Hold These Truths

"Because there is one loaf, we, who are many, are one body, for we all partake of the one loaf"

(1 Corinthians 10:17).

"So then, my brothers, when you come together to eat, wait for each other" (1 Corinthians 11:33).

The fourth day of every July reminds us that the United States of America was founded on the principle of independence. But the first day of every week reminds us that the church of the Lord Jesus Christ was founded on the principle of interdependence.

The document on which our country was founded, The Declaration of Independence, makes that principle very clear, in title and in content: "We hold these truths to be self-evident that all men are created equal; that they are endowed by their Creator with certain unalienable rights; that among these are life, liberty, and the pursuit of happiness."

But the document on which our church was founded, the New Testament, might well be called "The Declaration of Interdependence," a principle its contents make very clear. In fact we might sum up one of its great themes by saying, "We hold these truths to be evident in the revelation of Jesus Christ, that all

Christians are created in community; that they are endowed by their Creator with certain unalienable responsibilities; that among these are shared life, mutual service, and the pursuit of one another's holiness."

When we see red, white, and blue bunting and big parades, and star-spangled banners, we are reminded of our country's longing for independence. And when we gather to sing again to God and to one another, to offer our overheard prayers, and to express our mutual exhortations, we are reminded of our congregation's longing for interdependence.

We listen again to Paul: "Because there is one loaf, we, who are many, are one body" and "When you come together to eat, wait for each other." He reminds us that this meal, especially this meal, is our loud-as-a-firecracker-on the-Fourth-of-July Declaration of Interdependence.

God, we pray that our Communion here today might help us focus not only on the body of the Christ but also on the community of Christ.

Stay With Us

"Now that same day two of them were going to a village called Emmaus, about seven miles from Jerusalem. They were talking with each other about everything that had happened. As they talked and discussed these things with each other, Jesus himself came up and walked along with them; but they were kept from recognizing him. . . . As they approached the village to which they were going, Jesus acted as if he were going farther. But they urged him strongly, 'Stay with us, for it is nearly evening; the day is almost over.' So he went in to stay with them" (Luke 24:13-16, 28, 29).

They hadn't recognized him, as he traveled with them toward Emmaus.

They could easily have ignored his prying questions. They still hadn't recognized him, when he sculpted the Scriptures anew for them. They could easily have avoided his inspiring instruction.

But there was something about him that made them say, even insist, "Stay with us." And when he did, he became known to them in the breaking of the bread.

The risen Lord can be ignored, as he was by the other casual travelers who saw him on the road that day. They must have regarded him as just another accidental tourist.

And the risen Lord can be a source of temporary inspiration during a brief discouragement or disappointment. The Emmaus disciples could have let him go on, following with their eyes as they watched him walking wistfully away, receding in the dust and dusk of the evening. And in our minds we could do the same.

Or the risen Lord can be apprehended, even before we comprehend the full import of his identity, even if we never understand the full import of what he has done. Like the Emmaus disciples we may live in the lively hope that he will be known to us in the breaking of the bread.

And so we say, we insist, "Stay with us."

And he says, "This is my body broken for you. This cup is the new covenant in my blood, poured out for you." Which is another way of saying, "I will stay with you."

God, we pray that you stay with us, and open our eyes, so that we can sense what we cannot see.

Speaking His Language

"He came and preached peace to you who were far away and peace to those who were near. For through him we both have access to the Father by one Spirit. Consequently you are no longer foreigners and aliens, but fellow citizens with God's people and members of God's household" **(Ephesians 2:17-19).**

The traveler from the United States could read just enough Greek to find it in a list of churches in his hotel in Athens—Ekklesia Christou, "Church of Christ." He wrote down the address and handed it to a taxi driver. After a good deal more horn-honking than the light Sunday-morning traffic warranted, the driver pulled up to it on a relatively quiet side street. The traveler walked up to the converted second-story apartment over the Sunday-silent shop.

The welcome was warm, the prayers were earnest, the special music was heartfelt and melodic, and the sermon was obviously thoughtful and powerful. But even though the visitor had been able to read just enough Greek to locate this gathering of Christians half way across this walking-in-its-sleep city, halfway around the world from his not-yet-waking-from-its-sleep home congregation, he

understood nothing. Even the words at the
Lord's table were a mystery—no, not a mystery, which they always are in any language,
they were simply incomprehensible.

The mystery was that when the grizzled man
with the gnarled hands and gap-toothed grin
tore the bread and poured the cup and passed
among them with the emblems of the Lord's
body, the visitor suddenly comprehended the
crucified Christ. And he comprehended that
this meal needs no interpreter. This table is its
own translation.

When the visitor handed the emblems back,
the old man smiled. He was able to smile
because at last he was speaking a language the
visitor could understand.

*God, thank you for speaking our language in
Jesus, and for allowing us to speak each other's
languages in this meal.*

The Shadow of Death

"Now that same day two of them were going to a village called Emmaus, about seven miles from Jerusalem. They were talking with each other about everything that had happened. As they talked and discussed these things with each other, Jesus himself came up and walked along with them; but they were kept from recognizing him" (Luke 24:13-16).

It was resurrection day, but they were going home. It was resurrection day, but the Passover was past, and they were going home. It was resurrection day, but they were still hungover from the soberness of it all, with the three-day darkness of the crucifixion. It was resurrection day, but all they could talk about were the events of the last few days. They were stringing and restringing these days like dusky pearls that wouldn't hang together. They were remembering, rehearsing, reciting, repeating them, as if one more time through and it might all turn out differently: it might all make some sense.

Then they were joined by Jesus. But they didn't recognize him. Was it too dim in the fading light? Was it some supernatural stupor? Had they not known Jesus well? Had he changed? Were they tired or preoccupied?

Perhaps the reason was that these men, like

the twelve before them, were simply unable or
unwilling to process the paradox of a suffering
Messiah, a crucified Lord. They had been
unwilling to accept the fact that he with whom
they had lived could die. Now, in the same way
they seemed unable to accept the fact that he
who had died could be alive.

Is that why they could only, finally recognize
the risen Lord in the breaking of the bread, in
the tokens of his death? Can we recognize our
Lord in the same way?

*God, may these shadows of his death be for
us the evidences of his life, and ours.*

The Rending of Heaven

"As soon as Jesus was baptized, he went up out of the water. At that moment heaven was opened, and he saw the Spirit of God descending like a dove and lighting on him" (Matthew 3:16).
"And when Jesus had cried out again in a loud voice he gave up his spirit. At that moment the curtain of the temple was torn in two from top to bottom"
(Matthew 27:50, 51).

As Jesus was coming up out of the water, the dark and formless deep over which the Spirit had once hovered, the heavens themselves were torn open—the rending of Heaven. The physical barrier between the Father in Heaven and all humanity on earth was torn apart, while the Son of God was revealed as the Son of God.

Later, at Golgotha, a loud cry shook the foundations of the well-founded earth. The curtain of the temple, the sky-blue curtain stitched like the night sky with silver stars, the curtain that separated the heavenly, the Holy of Holies, from the earthly, was torn in two, from its heavenward top to its brush-the-earth bottom—the rending of Heaven. The ritual barrier between the Holy One and unholy humanity was torn apart, as the Son of God reconciled the children of God to God.

And when he took bread and broke it, there was no dove, no earthquake, just the ripping of the unleavened loaf—the rending of Heaven. The last barrier, the barrier of forgetfulness, between our "where-are-you" God and us hiding-in-the-garden humanity, is torn apart, the children of God remembering the Son of God. Do this in remembrance of him.

God, help us to remember your presence, your Heaven-rending, veil-rending, heart-rending presence.

Remembering
the Resurrection

"Remember Jesus Christ, raised from the dead"
(2 Timothy 2:8).

These are important words, "Remember Jesus Christ raised from the dead." They were spoken about the foundational fact of the Christian faith. They were spoken to the Christian evangelist Timothy to whom the gospel had been entrusted. And they were spoken by the great apostle Paul on the eve of his death.

These are also somewhat surprising words. Wouldn't Timothy have known all about the resurrection? Wouldn't the disciples Timothy ministered to have understood the meaning of the resurrection? Wasn't it the focus of their faith as it had been for Paul?

Yes, but Paul understood and Timothy and the Christians of Ephesus needed to understand that knowing and remembering are two different things. Of course they knew Jesus Christ raised from the dead. Now they needed to remember Jesus Christ, raised from the dead. And we also must know and remember the risen Christ in the same way.

When students get their test papers back,

they sometimes come up to the teacher's desk and ask for a correct answer. Frequently, when they hear it, their reaction is, "Oh I knew that; I just couldn't remember it." And teachers often respond, "If you can't remember it, then you didn't really know it." There is a sense in which that is true. But there is a sense in which knowing and remembering are two different things.

The resurrection of Jesus Christ from the dead is the most fundamental fact in all of human history. As Christians, as believers, we know that. But sometimes we don't remember it. Sometimes we don't think resurrection thoughts. Sometimes we don't maintain resurrection relationships. Sometimes we don't live resurrection lives. We too need Paul's admonition. "Remember Jesus Christ, raised from the dead."

But just how do we do that? We remember his resurrection best by remembering his death. That is why we have gathered on Sunday (Resurrection-remembrance Day) to remember his death. We remember his death until he, the one who could come again only by being raised from the dead, comes again.

God, we thank you for the reality of the resurrection in our lives, and for the way this remembrance of his saving death renews our memory of his victorious resurrection.

The Paradox
of His Presence

"Simon Peter asked him, 'Lord, where are you going?'
Jesus replied, 'Where I am going, you cannot follow
now, but you will follow later'"   (John 13:36).
"Before long, the world will not see me anymore, but
you will see me. Because I live, you also will live. On
that day you will realize that I am in my Father, and
you are in me, and I am in you"   (John 14:19, 20).
"And surely I am with you always to the very end of the
age"   (Matthew 28:20).

All of us have had the experience of adjust-
ing to the absence of someone we love. It may
have been the absence of a childhood friend
who moved away. Perhaps it was the death of a
parent. Or it could have been the occasion of a
son or daughter, brother or sister going off to
college.

When you walk through their room, you see
objects that remind you of them, and their
presence is real even in their absence. When
you perform some simple task, you remember
doing it with them or being taught how to do it
by them, and their presence is real even in
their absence. When you sit down for a meal,
you notice who is missing as much as who is
not missing. You notice those you tended to

take for granted, and their presence is real even in their absence. In fact, at times it might be truer to say, their presence is real especially in their absence.

It's the same at this table. It's the paradox of Jesus' statement, "Where I go you cannot follow me now" alongside his later assurance, "Surely, I am with you always." It's the paradox of his presence, that his presence is real even in his absence, perhaps especially in his absence.

So as we partake today, we notice his absence from the table. We think of Jesus apart from us, but more a part of us than if he were here with us. As we break the bread, we think, This is, not was, his body. And as we drink the cup, we remember, This is, not was, the cup of the new covenant in his blood.

God, help us to remember Jesus Christ. Help us handle his absence by celebrating his presence.

Objects in Mirror

"The Lord Jesus, on the night he was betrayed, took
bread, and when he had given thanks, he broke it and
said, 'This is my body, which is for you; do this in
remembrance of me'"   (1 Corinthians 11:23, 24).
"For where two or three come together in my name,
there am I with them"   (Matthew 18:20).
"For whenever you eat this bread and drink this cup,
you proclaim the Lord's death until he comes"

(1 Corinthians 11:26).

How is the Lord's Supper like driving a car?

No, this is not a trivia question. No, it's not
the lead-in to a joke. It's a serious question
with a serious answer.

How is the Lord's Supper like driving a car?

For one thing we are accelerating through a
rapidly passing present. And this meal calls us
to live purposefully and powerfully in the
midst of a present made meaningful by the
presence of Christ.

For another thing we feel the future flying
furiously in our face, speeding toward us like
the hurtling horizon. This meal forces us, frees
us, to face the future at whose boundary stands
a beckoning Christ.

And for yet another thing we catch ourselves
regularly, involuntarily, glancing in the

rearview mirror of a rapidly receding but always present past. And we are glancing in the right-sideview mirror where "Objects in mirror are closer than they appear." This meal lets us peek into a past full of Passovers stretching across the centuries where objects and actions, people and promises are closer, much closer, than they appear.

This meal is a mental magnet for our mind's eye. It reflects from the rear the rush of redemption, gaining ground on us, the past passing us and becoming our redemptive future.

God, help us to see in the bread and cup the past, present, and future of the salvation that we find only in you.

Zero Degrees Longitude

"Let us run with perseverance the race marked out for us. Let us fix our eyes on Jesus the author and perfecter of our faith who for the joy set before him endured the cross, scorning its shame, and sat down at the right hand of the throne of God"

(Hebrews 12:1, 2).

It is somewhat less than you might expect, less a work of art, less a wonder of technology, sitting there at the place and time where time and place are set. We speak of the observatory on top of the hill-and-nothing-more in Greenwich, England.

No less earthly or earthy, no less odd or old, no less worn by foot and finger as they traced the track, is the artificial line on your globe. That line leaps from under your finger to this unspecial spot on the unlined face of the earth in Greenwich, England. This is zero degrees longitude.

The observatory at Greenwich may be relatively unimpressive. But the person who visits is nevertheless impressed. He is a better person after having stood in Greenwich, England, at zero degrees longitude. Somehow he is more secure about starting, starting over, starting out, on this planet, on this journey, on this self.

And that is where we stand this day in this place, this here-and-now, at this table (no work of art, no wonder of technology), and among these people (no work of art, no wonder of technology). It is somewhat less than we might expect, this no-less-earthly, no-less-earthy, no-less-odd-or-old act, but it makes us some-how more secure about starting, starting over, starting out, on our journey, on ourselves. We are better people after having stood around this table, the Lord's table, our zero degrees longitude.

God, we pray that you give us the courage to begin anew every time we end up at this our starting point.

What's-your-name?

"Now that same day two of them were going to a village called Emmaus, about seven miles from Jerusalem. . . . When he was at the table with them, he took bread, gave thanks, broke it and began to give it to them. Then their eyes were opened and they recognized him" (Luke 24:13, 30, 31).

How strange of Luke to leave out one of the names. Luke, was the Gospel writer who above all the others wanted to record historical details. He identified the current emperor, governor, and king. He named Zechariah and Elizabeth, Simeon and Anna, Lazarus the beggar, Zacchaeus the publican, even blind Bartimaeus. But oddly he named only one of the two on the road to Emmaus—Cleopas and . . . and . . . what's-his-name.

But how absolutely predictable of Luke to highlight this story of the risen Lord appearing to two such unknown, almost anonymous travelers to Emmaus. We have no idea who they were or what they knew, thought, or believed about Jesus. We do not know where the road to Emmaus was, or even where Emmaus was, for that matter.

For Luke, telling the story of these unknowns who knew Jesus in the breaking of the bread was just the point.

The Son of God died for us, the crucified Christ rose for us. He did that for nameless, faceless people like us. Jesus came, died, and rose for the what's-their-names of the world, so that the simplest of people might recognize him in the simplest of actions, in the breaking of the bread.

This is his body broken for . . . for . . . what's-your-name. This is the cup of the new covenant in his blood, poured out for . . . for . . . what's-your-name.

God, thank you for giving Jesus the name that is above every name, so that every anonymous knee, including our own, might bow before him.

Scriptural Index

Topical Index

Seasonal Index